Paul Klee

Animal Tricks

Prestel

The Twittering Machine

Are these supposed to be birds?

At first glance they look a bit like clothes horses.
They don't really have bodies but just lines.
One thing though is quite clear—they're twittering!
Life's good, and they're telling us so. Chirping away
to their heart's content, with their beaks wide open and
their long tongues a-waggling. A chorus of bird-song!

Paul Klee liked painting animals in his pictures.
Before he started he often did a drawing first,
as he has done here.

He called this one *Concert on a Branch.*

But where are the birds in the picture on the facing
page actually sitting? On a branch in the countryside?
Not really—it looks more like a raised platform with
a music stand on it.

And what's that peculiar handle on the right?
Perhaps it's a handle used to wind up an old record player.

In fact it's a machine—Klee's *Twittering Machine*. This is the name the artist himself wrote on the
picture. A machine, like something in a factory. The title gives the picture a whole new meaning.
Klee often did that. He nearly always gave his pictures titles—he called it 'christening' them.
The titles show what his thoughts were and what things he liked.

Music was very important to Klee. Before deciding to become an artist,

he even thought of being a musician. In fact he often painted pictures about singers, dancers
and musicians. And many of his pictures reflect another of his passions: animals—animals singing,
twittering, or even roaring!

1922 / 151   Die Zwitscher-Maschine

Bird Encounter

Klee didn't turn birds just into machines.
Sometimes he painted birds high in the sky,
way above the rooftops. What are they doing there?
Well, of course they're standing around and talking!
Don't these two look like people who've bumped
into each other and are having a chat?

"Lovely day today,"
the one on the right might be saying.

This picture was painted earlier than *The Twittering Machine*.
Klee was still painting birds with bodies then. The only
odd thing is, they're not flying. They're standing there with
their wings tucked back. But where are they? Is it somewhere
in the countryside? Perhaps not, as the ground is nowhere
to be seen.

The birds seem to hover in the air.

Below them there are some areas of colour—a crescent moon,
a star, and two roofs.

It's very typical of Klee to suggest surroundings just with patches of colour.
He often did this. The first time was in 1914, when he went to North Africa with two painter
friends, August Macke and Louis Moilliet. It's particularly clear in his camel picture
which you will find on page 13.

4

1918/202 Vogel - Begegnung

Some birds are flying in Klee's pictures, like the lark here. You can also make out a landscape with trees, houses, hills and the sun—or perhaps there are even two suns? And in the middle is the outline of a bird soaring upwards. It is a lark, as the title says.

But couldn't it just as easily be an eagle, like in the other picture called With the Eagle? Even the countryside is similar in the two pictures—bathed in an orange light, like at sunset.

With the Lark Ascending

This is also a puzzling painting! A deer can be seen and a little cat is hiding in there somewhere. But what does the eye mean which can be seen under the arch in the middle? Who are the little figures at the bottom? Is that a soldier standing in front of the house?

When he painted these two pictures in 1918, Klee had just returned from fighting in World War I. He had been a soldier for two years. Although he had drawn and painted throughout that period, he was now able to turn to painting again, and could work on bigger pictures once more.

Forest Fowl

What a red picture! But here the bird is on the ground, running along as if it can't fly at all! And where have all the trees gone? Once again we can only make a guess as to where the bird is. There are patches of red and outlines of trees here and there. It's a wood full of different shades of red.

As in *Bird Encounter* on page 5, areas and space are only hinted at by patches of colour. But here the edges are sharp and the patches are quite separate. It's not really possible to make out a real place in the country.

Only in the top left of the picture can we see a few rough branches. As in some of Klee's other pictures, it is the effect of one particular colour that is most important—in this case it is the colour red.

Red dominates the whole picture.

1920.81. Waldvogel.

Brocard Cat Washing

Klee didn't only paint birds—although birds do appear quite often in his pictures. Really he was a cat fan! He adored cats and often drew or painted them. He had several during his lifetime; the last one was a Persian cat called Bimbo. Klee used to talk 'Bimbo lingo' to him.

This picture on the facing page shows another cat. It's a special breed called a Brocard, which has red and grey spots on white fur. She has twisted herself around as only cats can do, and is washing and grooming herself.

This is one of Klee's early paintings. It was done long before the other pictures we've looked at so far. He used just a handful of delicate colours—whites, dark greys, a greyish brown and an orangey red. He painted with big brushstrokes and, with just a few spots of colour and carefully-drawn lines, brought it to life.

At first, Klee mainly did drawings in black, white and grey washes and watercolours, as he found it difficult to paint pictures in colour. To keep down the cost of his first experiments with colour, he drew and painted on panes of glass. He then simply washed a lot of his pictures off the glass if he didn't like them. But he must have liked this picture of the Brocard cat, because he kept it!

With the Brown

How did Klee get the idea to paint like this several years later? Why didn't he paint a normal landscape, showing the world as it really is, with animals, trees and houses, just as we know them? It's all to do with his journey to North Africa in 1914. In Tunisia things look quite different than back home. The bright light and the heat make colours and shapes gleam and shimmer. Objects look like shining patches in the sun, while shadows are a deep black or blue. On this journey, Klee got the impression that not only the countryside, but also animals—or in fact anything—can be painted as an area of colour.

He painted this picture when he was back home in Munich. It shows a camel set in a landscape of stripes. It's made up of lots of bright reds, a dab of yellow and brown, and a bit of purple and watery grey. Klee was mainly interested in how light and shade effects different colours. In one spot, the red gleams brightly in the sun, in another it is dark and heavy in the shade. This is why he worked very hard to get not just the right shade of each colour but also the right brightness.

"And Another Camuff," Klee wrote on a drawing that also shows a camel. It almost looks as if he had tried to draw the animal in one continuous line, without lifting his pencil from the paper. The word 'camuff' comes from Italian *camuffo*, which means 'rascal.' In Berne, where Klee grew up, it refers to someone who is not very clever. And you have to admit, this camel doesn't look very intelligent, does it?

1915. 39.

13

Picture with the Cock and the Grenadier

The cockerel near the top of the picture is almost lost in its surroundings. It is not very big, but even so is bigger than the soldier—the grenadier—at the bottom. In this painting, there are no stripes like in the camel picture, just light and dark rectangles put together, bits of a landscape scene and various other things that don't really belong anywhere. You can make out a window, with a door beside it, then an archway on the left edge. And individual trees are dotted about all over the place.

This is a large painting, not a watercolour like the other pictures we have seen so far. After World War I, Klee became very successful. It gave him confidence in himself, encouraging him to paint in oils. Previously he had always shied away from painting in oil, preferring to draw smaller pictures or paint watercolours.

The colours are different now as well. Klee painted mainly using dark colours—with lots of **black** and **dark green**—placing a few bright, gleaming spots of strong colour between them. Everything in the watercolours he painted on his journey to Tunisia was light and bright; now the colours are dark and heavy. But one thing is the same— he created a feeling of space in the picture using colour alone. There is no sense of perspective, no lines that indicate depth or a defined area. He is simply using colour.

Travelling Birds

These birds with their big eyes remind us of those in *The Twittering Machine* on page 3, don't they?
This picture was completed just before it. The lines are blurred—frayed, spotted and dotted here, too.
There isn't even one really sharp line—in fact, that wouldn't really have been possible using this technique.

Klee drew both pictures in the same way. First he made a drawing, then he coated one side of a sheet of paper with paint and slid this between the drawing and a blank sheet, with the side with the black oil paint facing down. He traced over the drawing and this is the result. It is called an 'oil transfer' and was a new technique that Klee developed himself. He traced the lines onto single-coloured but not necessarily even surfaces.

The result was a picture full of light.

For the first time, the birds seem to really fly.
Are they just flapping around or are they going somewhere?

They are simply on the move—where to is not so important and we'll never know for sure.

As so often with Klee, this picture still leaves us with some unanswered questions. But that's what he wanted.

"Do we need to know everything?
I don't really think so,"

he wrote on one of his last pictures.

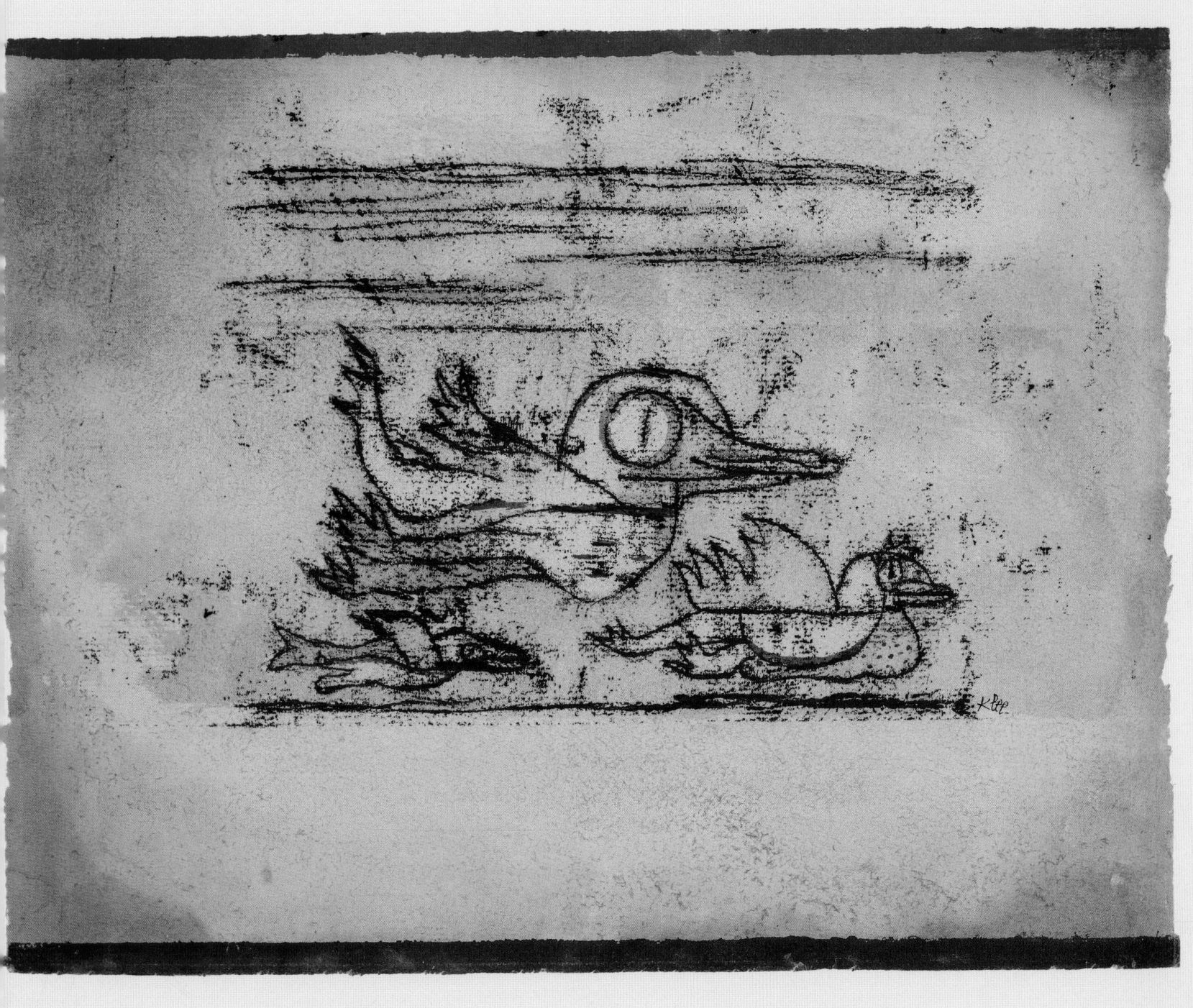

Crow Landscape

There's no more flying into the distance or lightness here. This is the land of dark-coloured birds. *Crow Landscape* is the title of the picture.

Landscape?

There are just a few areas of colour and one or two lines. And yet they're all there—the trees, the hills and the sun. You can still make out the landscape quite easily. And what are the crows doing? Are they simply strolling around the place or are they strutting attentively, keeping an eye on everything?

Klee painted this very large picture when he was teaching at an important art school in Germany, the Bauhaus in Dessau. One of the things that he was very interested in was the question of harmony and balance in painting. That is why he chose to use a lot of similar shades of colour here—reds and browns and a little white, and placed the crows symmetrically in opposite corners. Other parts of the picture show the same harmony and balance, don't they?

Where Eggs Come From
...and the Juicy Joint

What a wonderful title for a picture!
How did Paul Klee think up that?

It actually fits the subject very well.
The picture solves the riddle. You really can see

an egg and a hen ...

... and a pig.

How did he draw this picture? We've already seen dotted lines like these before in other pictures. Here too, Klee took a drawing and traced it, as he did in *The Twittering Machine* and *Travelling Birds* on pages 3 and 17.

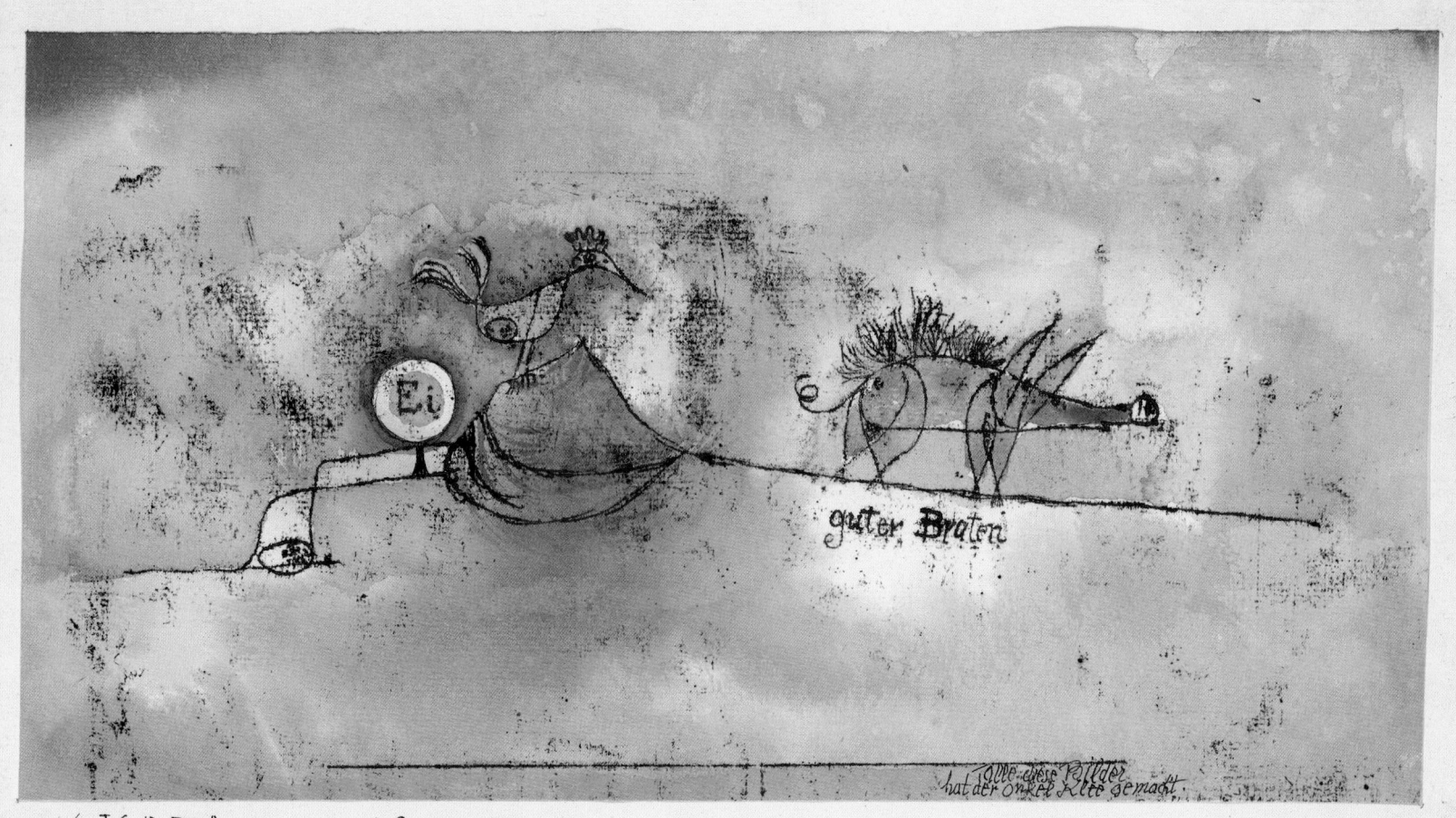

1921/6 Wo die Eier herkommen und der gute Braten (für Florina-Irene)

Paul Klee really wanted to dream up something funny for his godchild Florina-Irene. She was the daughter of a couple of musicians who were very close friends of his. Florina-Irene was seriously ill at the time, so 'Uncle Klee' painted this picture for her. To cheer her up explained where eggs and the Sunday roast come from!

'All these pictures have been done by Uncle Klee'

21

Klee painted another picture as a present
for Florina-Irene. He called it *Animal Tricks*.

Is it a circus menagerie?

It must have been some circus show! All those different animals in the ring together.
The one leading the way looks like a donkey. What could that be riding it, with a whip
in its paw? And is that a dog just behind them? A creature with wings is doing gymnastics
on its back and can keep its balance without any problems.

But it doesn't look like a circus, does it? There isn't a ring or an audience.
Just a broken line to mark the ground where the animals are walking.
They have come along to show off their tricks to Florina-Irene—

it's a special performance just for her.

Animal Tricks

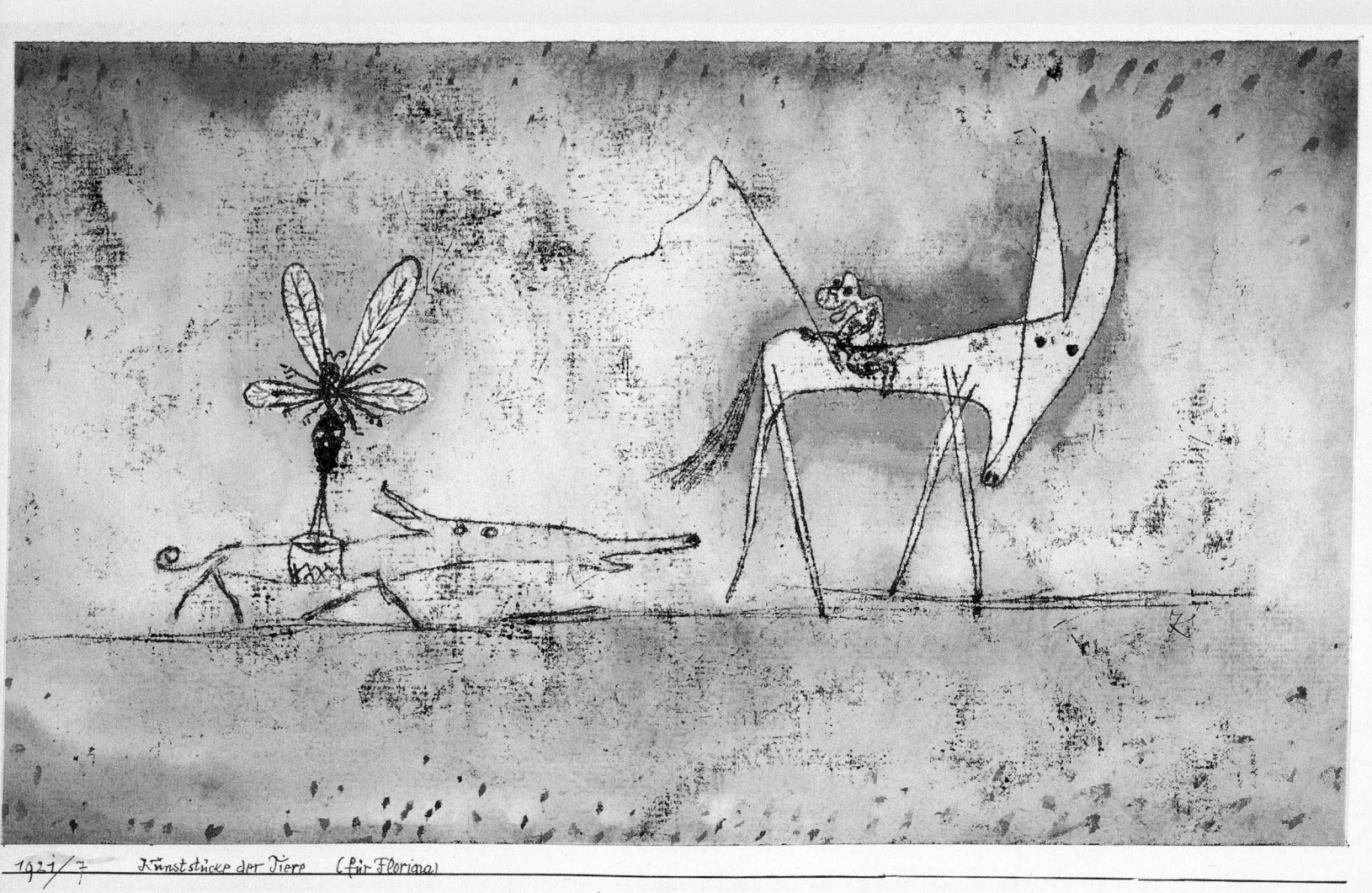

1921/7   Künststücke der Tiere   (für Floriana)

Fish Picture

Other animals can do tricks, too. Don't you think it looks as if the fish are dancing in this picture? Or perhaps they are just playing.

The fish are scattered right across the picture and are always on the move. They seem to stick closely to each other even though they have split in two little groups.

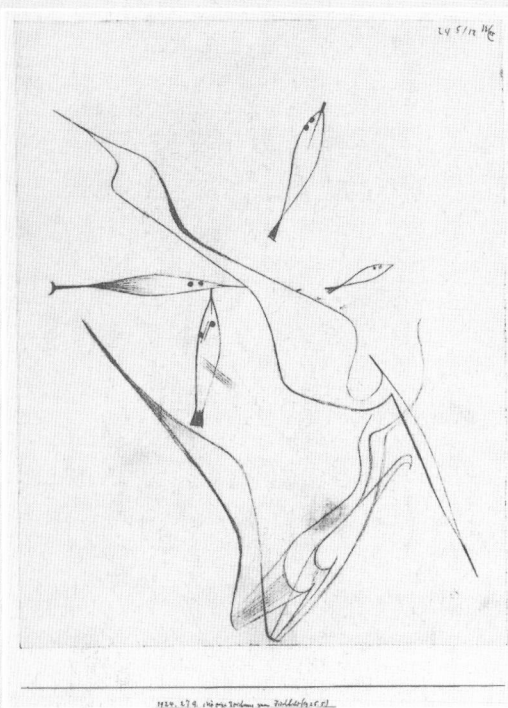

Klee first drew the groups independently of one another, making two drawings. He called the drawings

The First Drawing for the Fish Picture

and

The Other Drawing for the Fish Picture.

When he wrote down their titles, he obviously knew he'd get them all dancing together!

The deep blue in the picture is like in an aquarium.

Oddly, not just the picture itself is blue—Klee painted part of the frame blue as well. For him, the picture was not just a piece of painted cloth. To put this idea across, he took the material he'd painted and fixed it onto cardboard and then framed it. After that he painted the cardboard and inner part of the frame blue. This has a different effect from a normal picture—somehow more closed and inward-looking. Watertight, perhaps!

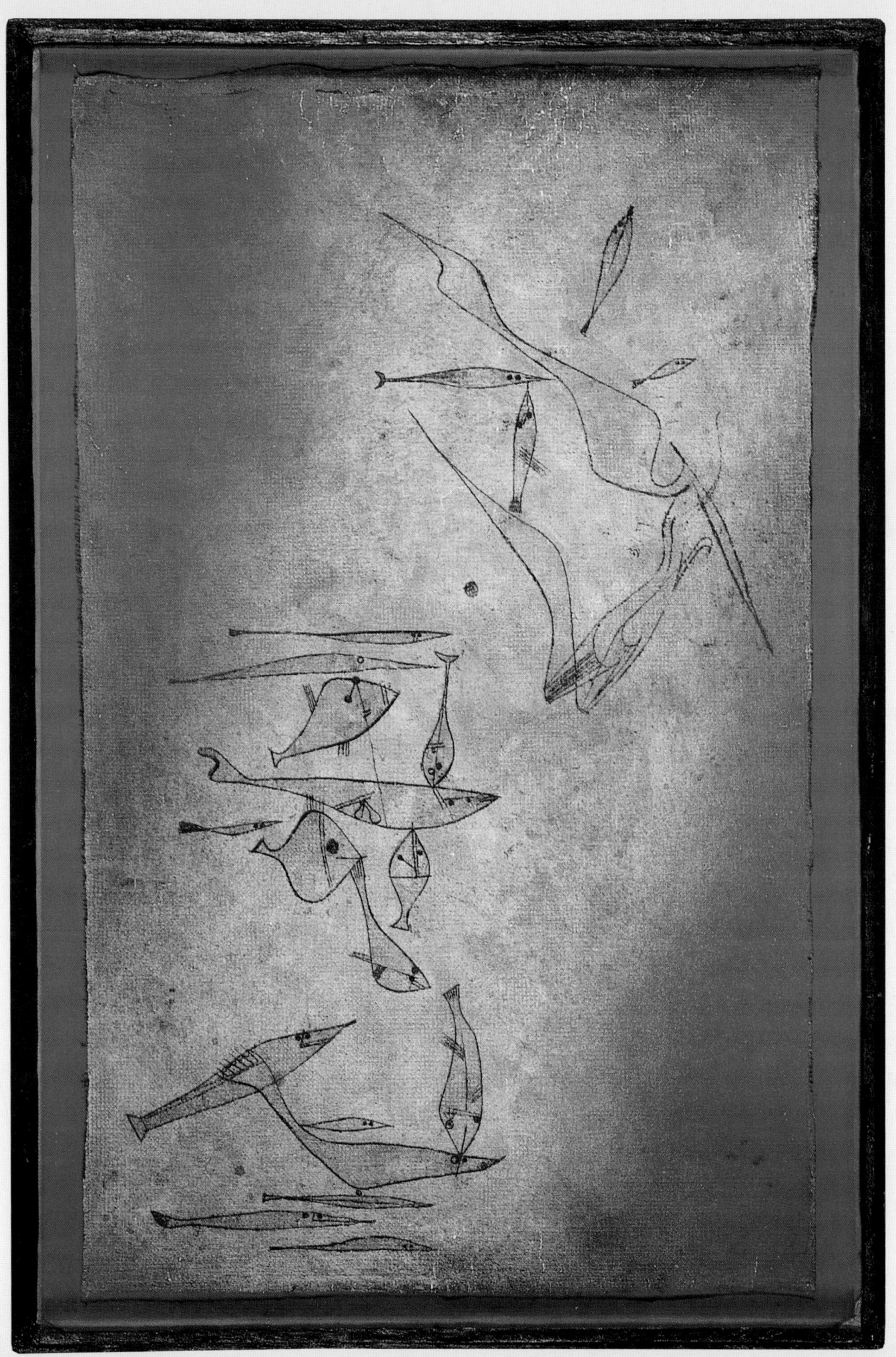

Doesn't it look as if a gentle breeze has just blown these animals onto the picture—they seem so delicate and weightless? The almost colourless bodies of the two animals are made up of just a few lines and dots. Klee drew their outlines in one go, almost without lifting his pencil.

But what kind of animals are they? A duck and an antelope, perhaps? It really isn't very important. What matters more is that the animals are moving closer to each other; they seem to be getting along together and are pleased to have met up. Although they don't look like humans, these two animals are behaving rather like them.

That's quite typical of Klee. He liked to show his animals' state of mind—whether they were sad or happy.

Once again, Klee used the oil transfer technique. However, unlike in other pictures, he created the background to this painting. He drew the animals and painted the bluish-pink sky and turquoise ground in watercolour. This picture looks quite different from *The Twittering Machine*, for example. Despite their delicacy, the two animals have well-defined bodies, even though some of the dots do not actually belong.

Klee seldom used the oil transfer technique later on. Instead, he turned more and more to drawing and painting.

Shortly before working on this picture, he gave up his job at the Bauhaus and accepted another job a long way away, in Düsseldorf. But he still kept in touch with his friends in Dessau as his wife stayed on there for a while. Whenever he went back to see her, he could meet up with his friends too.

Animal Friendship

Paul Klee's Biography

Paul Klee was born on 18 December, 1879 in Switzerland, and grew up in Berne.

Five-year old Paul with his sister Mathilde, who was three years older

He liked writing poetry and music as much as painting. However, in the end, he decided in favour of painting, After leaving school, he moved to Munich in Germany in 1899 to study painting.

In 1902, he spent six months travelling around Italy, before returning to Berne. As he could not make a living from selling his pictures, he worked as a musician.

In 1906, he married the pianist Lily Stumpf and went back with her to Munich, where she came from. A year later, their son Felix was born.

Paul Klee (far right) as leading violin in the string quintet at the Von Knirr School of Drawing in Munich. The easels were used as music stands.

Paul and Lily Klee (1932)

In Munich, he got to know the painters August Macke and Wassily Kandinsky. Through them, he became involved with the famous Blue Rider group of artists.

Around this time, he began to draw up a catalogue in which he kept notes and numbered all his works. He kept up this catalogue with unremitting precision to the day he died, recording more than 9,000 pictures in it!

At Easter 1914, Klee and Macke went to Tunisia with another painter, Louis Moilliet. The trip had major consequences for Klee's painting. There, he developed a different approach to colour and subsequently changed his style completely.

The next four years were dominated by World War I. Like many other artists, Klee had to do military service, and was only demobbed in 1918.

Around this time he had his first major successes. Eventually, in 1920, he got a job teaching at the Bauhaus in Weimar. The Bauhaus was not just an academy of painting. Its aim was to bring together all the arts (architecture, painting, sculpture, crafts). When the Bauhaus moved to nearby Dessau four years later, Klee moved with it.

In 1931, Klee was appointed professor at the Academy of Art in Düsseldorf. In 1933, he was sacked from his job by the National Socialists. His ideas about painting were so different from theirs. At the end of the year he moved back to Berne in Switzerland.

Paul and Felix Klee on the balcony of the flat in Berne (1934)

Around 1937, Klee went down with a serious skin disease from which he never recovered. It also made working sometimes difficult for him. Nevertheless, he went on painting and drawing. In 1939, he managed to paint 1,253 works, but in the following year he painted or drew only 366 before he had to go to Locarno in the Tessin region of Switzerland for treatment that June, where he died on 29 June 1940 at the age of sixty-one.

View of the exhibition called 'Decadent' art, held by the National Socialists—first in Munich, then in other cities. It included all the pictures that were considered too modern or did not conform with what the Nazis considered as art. Seventeen of Klee's pictures were included, notably *The Twittering Machine*. Subsequently, this picture, which belonged to the National Gallery in Berlin at the time, was seized along with 106 other paintings, drawings and watercolours from German museums.

Many of the pictures condemned by the National Socialists were destroyed. But although they considered the pictures to be inferior and had forbidden anyone to exhibit them, as well as banning the artists, this did not stop the Nazis selling a lot of pictures abroad. That's how *The Twittering Machine* was saved. With the help of dealers, it reached New York. It's now on show there as one of the Museum of Modern Art's most famous pictures.